PARKER Vic   X - 2006.
G.R.R Writer   Heinemann
(Writers Uncovered)   £ 11.99

DATE DUE

0 9 SEP 2009		

Writers Uncovered

J.R.R. TOLKIEN

Vic Parker

Heinemann
LIBRARY

www.heinemann.co.uk/library
Visit our website to find out more information about Heinemann Library books.

To order:
☎ Phone 44 (0) 1865 888066
📄 Send a fax to 44 (0) 1865 314091
💻 Visit the Heinemann bookshop at www.heinemann.co.uk/library to browse
our catalogue and order online.

First published in Great Britain by
Heinemann Library, Halley Court, Jordan Hill,
Oxford OX2 8EJ, part of Harcourt Education.

Heinemann is a registered trademark of
Harcourt Education Ltd.

Editorial: Charlotte Guillain and Dave Harris
Design: Richard Parker and Q2A Solutions
Picture research: Hannah Taylor and
    Andrea Sadler
Production: Duncan Gilbert

Originated by Chroma Graphics (O) Pte Ltd
Printed and bound in China by
    South China Printing Company

10 digit ISBN: 0 431 90626 2
13 digit ISBN: 978 0 431 90626 3

10 09 08 07 06
10 9 8 7 6 5 4 3 2 1

British Library Cataloguing in Publication Data
Parker, Vic
    J.R.R. Tolkien. – (Writers uncovered)
    823.9'12
A full catalogue record for this book is
available from the British Library.

Acknowledgements
The publishers would like to thank the
following for permission to reproduce
photographs:
Alamy Images p. **12** (Oxford Picture Library);
Ancient Art & Architecture Collection p. **11**
(M Jelliffe); Billett Potter pp. **4**, **27**, **39**;
Birmingham Public Libraries pp. **6**, **8**;
Camera Press pp. **42** (Stewart Mark), **21**;
Corbis Royalty Free p. **13**; Harcourt Education
Ltd pp. **16**, **18** (Tudor Photography);
HarperCollins pp. **29**, **31**, **33**, **34**, **35**; Leeds
University p. **17**; Mary Evans Picture Library
pp. **10**, **25**; Motoring Picture Library p. **19**;
Photograph courtesy of the Fathers of the
Birmingham Oratory p. **9**; Ronald Grant/
New Line Cinema p. **37**; The Art Archive
p. **7** (Oldsaksammlung Oslo/Dagli Orti);
Topham Picturepoint pp. **15**, **22**; Used by
permission of The Marion E. Wade Center,
Wheaton College, Wheaton, IL. pp. **20**, **23**.

Every effort has been made to contact
copyright holders of any material reproduced
in this book. Any omissions will be rectified
in subsequent printings if notice is given to
the publishers.

The paper used to print this book comes
from sustainable resources.

CONTENTS

Words appearing in the text in bold, **like this**, are explained in the glossary.

Have you heard of Gandalf the wizard, Bilbo and Frodo Baggins the hobbits, and Arwen the Elf? They are all beloved characters created by the Oxford University professor, J.R.R. Tolkien. Tolkien's first novel, *The Hobbit*, was published in 1937, but is as enchanting today as it was then. *The Lord of the Rings*, which continues the story of *The Hobbit*, is considered by many people to be the finest work of **fantasy** in English literature.

Tolkien's life's work, *The Silmarillion*, is a huge **mythology** which is as wide-ranging and fascinating as the Norse legends of Ancient Iceland. Tolkien was truly a master **myth**-maker and **linguist**. He invented an entire world where humans, hobbits, dwarves, elves, and wizards are caught up in age-long struggles between the forces of darkness and light. His heroes must find and destroy magical treasures and fight terrible battles.

The face behind the stories.

What was Tolkien like?

Tolkien was a rather short, ordinary-looking **middle-class** Englishman. He wore plain, sensible clothes typical of the times he lived in, such as sturdy brown shoes, tweed jackets, and flannel trousers. However, towards the end of his life when he had become rich from his books, he spent his money on coloured waistcoats.

Tolkien was a down-to-earth person, and he found it easy to strike up conversations with people and make friends. He spoke very quickly, because thoughts were always quickly crowding his brain. Tolkien had a great sense of humour and liked playing practical jokes. Most of all, he liked relaxing in the company of close friends, discussing ancient writing and sharing ideas for stories.

FIND OUT MORE...

Here are some of J.R.R. Tolkien's favourites:

Favourite food...	Plain English food – Tolkien hated fancy French cooking.
Favourite hobbies...	Tending his roses and looking after his lawn.
Favourite plant...	Tolkien loved trees. They often feature in his stories, such as the forests of Fangorn and Lothlorien.
Favourite sport...	As a schoolboy, Tolkien was an excellent rugby player.
Favourite car...	Tolkien's first car was a Morris Cowley which he nicknamed "Jo".

John Ronald Reuel Tolkien was born on 3 January 1892. His parents, called Mabel and Arthur, came from Birmingham, England, but had set up home in South Africa. They had travelled there so Arthur could get a job as a bank manager. On 17 February 1894, they had another son, called Hilary Arthur Reuel.

A sad start

Mabel found it difficult to bring up her babies in the South African heat. In those days, there were monkeys, snakes, and poisonous spiders in their garden, and wild dogs and lions roaming the plains around their town. In April 1895, she sailed with the boys back to England for a long holiday with her family. Arthur was meant to join them soon, but important work matters kept stopping him from travelling. Then in November he fell ill and could not travel. On 15 February 1896, he died. Tolkien was just four years old.

New beginnings

Mabel faced poverty. She found a tiny cottage to rent in a village outside Birmingham, called Sarehole. There were hardly any other houses or traffic, and Tolkien loved exploring the countryside with his brother. The meadows, woods and rivers stimulated his imagination.

Living in the Sarehole countryside, it was hard to believe that the big industrial city of Birmingham was close by.

When Tolkien came across a grumpy local **miller** and farmer he nicknamed them the "White and Black Ogres". Tolkien had plenty of time for adventuring, because Mabel gave him school lessons at home. He could read by age four, and began to learn Latin and French too.

FIND OUT MORE...

Tolkien loved books, particularly Native American adventure tales, fairy stories of magic and goblins such as the "Curdie" books of George Macdonald, and legends, such as tales of King Arthur. His favourite story was a Viking legend about a dragon called Fafnir, slain by a hero called Sigurd.

This Viking carving shows Sigurd killing Fafnir the dragon with his sword.

Starting school

When Tolkien was eight, he passed an exam to go to a top private school for boys in Birmingham, called King Edward's. A kind uncle paid the fees. The school was in the city centre, four miles from Sarehole. Tolkien had to walk, because his mother could not afford the train fare.

Soon, Mabel decided they had to move from their lovely countryside cottage into the smoky, dingy city. For a while they rented a house next to a railway line. Then they moved close to a large church which Mabel attended, called the Birmingham Oratory.

INSIDE INFORMATION

Tolkien's mother sometimes took him and his brother to visit their cousins, Mary and Marjorie Incledon. Tolkien and Mary invented their own language, Nevbosh, and made up limericks in it. They made up their own "nonsense" words by changing regular English words, and also used some ideas from French and Latin.

Birmingham is Britain's second largest city. This is what the city centre looked like when Tolkien was a boy.

Tragedy strikes

In April 1904, Mabel developed an illness called diabetes. Today, diabetes is treatable, but in those days the right medicines had not been discovered. She became very sick and, in November, she died. Tolkien was twelve and an orphan.

A kind, wealthy priest at the Birmingham Oratory, Father Francis Morgan, became guardian to Tolkien and his brother. He paid for the boys to live in the house of a distant relative. However, from then on, they spent a lot of time at the Oratory, eating meals with the priests, playing there, and reading from Father Francis's library. Each summer, Father Francis took the boys on holiday to the seaside at Lyme Regis. Tolkien enjoyed exploring the countryside and sketching the scenery. He became excellent at drawing and painting.

Father Francis Morgan was a kind guardian to Tolkien and his brother.

A love of languages

When Tolkien lived by the railway line, he enjoyed spotting mysterious, magical-sounding Welsh names on coal-trucks. He liked learning another language at school: Greek. He was also fascinated when a teacher read Geoffrey Chaucer's *Canterbury Tales* aloud in **Medieval** English. Tolkien began to devour books that taught ancient languages, such as Anglo-Saxon and Gothic. He mastered an Anglo-Saxon poem about a monster-slaying hero called *Beowulf*, and an **Arthurian** legend in Medieval English called *Sir Gawain and the Green Knight*. He even learned the story of Fafnir and Sigurd in its original language, Old Icelandic.

This illustration shows the hero, Beowulf (on the right), travelling to kill the monster, Grendel.

HAVE A GO

Tolkien developed an interest in artistic lettering, known as calligraphy. Many years later, he used decorative, old-fashioned lettering styles in maps for his stories. You can try doing this yourself with pens that have special calligraphy nibs.

A firm friend

Tolkien found a friend at school, Christopher Wiseman, who was also keen on languages. Christopher was particularly captivated by the strange alphabet of Egyptian **hieroglyphics**. Tolkien became engrossed in his spare time creating new alphabets and languages of his own.

A forbidden love

When Tolkien was sixteen, Father Francis moved him and his brother to a bigger, more pleasant lodging house. He thought this would help Tolkien to study for a prize called a **scholarship** to go to Oxford University. However, over the next couple of years, instead of working hard, Tolkien fell in love with another lodger. She was a girl three years older than him called Edith Bratt. When Father Francis found out, he was furious. He moved the boys to new accommodation and ordered Tolkien not to see or write to Edith until he was 21 years old.

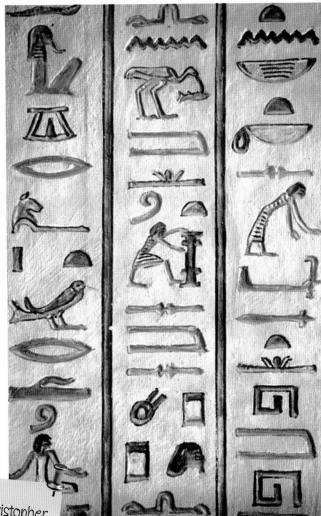

Tolkien's friend Christopher Wiseman was fascinated by the way Egyptian hieroglyphics used pictures and symbols to represent words and sounds.

Eighteen-year-old Tolkien was deeply upset about losing Edith, but he had close friends at school to cheer him up, including Christopher Wiseman, Robert Gilson, and Geoffrey Smith. They met regularly at the restaurant of a shop called Barrow's Stores to read poetry over afternoon tea. They called themselves the TCBS, which was made up of the initial letters from "Tea Club" and "Barrovian Society". Tolkien also started writing poetry of his own.

Off to Oxford

Tolkien succeeded in winning an entrance prize to Oxford University, and in October 1911 he went to part of the university called Exeter College to study for a degree in **Classics**. He later changed to an English degree, because this allowed him to specialise in his favourite languages, such as Anglo-Saxon, Old Icelandic, and Old Finnish. While Tolkien was at university, he turned 21. He lost no time in making contact with Edith again and soon the couple were engaged.

Another writer who has more recently studied at Exeter College is Philip Pullman.

One of Tolkien's poems, called *Goblin Feet*, was published in a collection. Tolkien spent most of his time out and about with his friends, or working on his private languages and composing his own poetry. He also experimented with writing stories. Despite spending a lot of time writing rather than studying, Tolkien did excellently in his studies. In 1914, he won an award called the Skeat Prize, and in his final exams he got a First – the top, rarely-awarded grade.

Tolkien wanted a career as a university teacher, while also trying to earn some money from his poetry. However, he had to put all his plans on hold. World War I had started and all young men like Tolkien were needed to go and fight.

INSIDE INFORMATION

Between leaving school and starting university, Tolkien went on a holiday in the mountains of Switzerland with his brother. He bought some postcards, one of which was a picture of an old, white-bearded man called "the mountain spirit". Tolkien loved this picture and said that it inspired him to create the wizard character, Gandalf. The dramatic Swiss mountains could also have inspired some of the landscapes in *The Lord of the Rings*.

Army training

Straight after finishing university, in July 1915, Tolkien joined an army regiment called the Lancashire Fusiliers. He was sent on training to learn army drill, battle tactics, and weapons techniques. Tolkien decided to put his interest in languages to good use by specialising in signalling. He learned how to work with messaging systems such as **Morse code**, flag and lamp signalling, and even carrier pigeons. Finally, he became the batallion's signalling officer.

Facing the front line

Tolkien would soon be sent to war. So many soldiers were dying on the battlefield, he knew that he might well never return. He decided there was no time to waste in marrying Edith, and the couple had a quiet wedding on 22 March 1916. Tolkien also tried to get a selection of his poems published by sending them to a company called Sidgwick & Jackson. Unfortunately, they were rejected and he did not have time to try any other publishers. On 4 June 1916, he was sent to France.

FIND OUT MORE...

World War I lasted from 1914 to 1918. It came about because of tensions that had been growing for many years between two sets of European **allies**: Germany, Austria, and Hungary on one side, and Britain, France, and Russia on the other. It is sometimes called "the Great War" because around 15 million people died, and it involved more countries at a larger scale than any other war before.

Into battle

Tolkien found himself in mud-filled **trenches**, bombarded day and night by machine-gun fire and explosions. Many of his battalion were horribly injured or killed. Dead bodies lay everywhere on the battlefield. Tolkien managed to stay alive, but at the end of October he was stricken with an illness called **trench fever**. He was sent back to hospital in England.

The trenches of World War I battlefields were knee-deep in water and overrun by rats. Soldiers had to live and fight in these appalling conditions, and the terrible experience must have influenced Tolkien's later writing.

The end of Tolkien's war

Tolkien was reunited with Edith and, when he was well enough, he went to her lodgings in Great Haywood, Staffordshire, to recover gradually. The couple were thrilled when a baby son was born in November 1917. They called him John Francis Reuel. But times were tragic too. Tolkien's school friends Robert Gilson and Geoffrey Smith both died in the war. Tolkien determined to honour their memory by writing a book similar to the great, heroic legends they all loved.

A LIFE OF WRITING AND TEACHING

Tolkien set himself a massive task: to create an entire mythological world, with its own landscapes and creatures, several languages, and a complete history. He began composing legends for it, knowing that it would take years to write. He first called the project "The Book of Lost Tales", but later retitled it *The Silmarillion*.

Embarking on a career

Tolkien's trench fever kept coming and going, and he never became fit enough to return to the front line. Fortunately, the war ended in November 1918. Now Tolkien had to find a job. He used old university contacts to find work in Oxford, putting together the New English Dictionary. Soon, he was able to give this up because colleges started sending him English students to teach. Meanwhile, in his spare time, he continued writing.

Tolkien lived on this street in Oxford.

A move to Leeds

In the summer of 1920, a specialist English Language teaching job became available at Leeds University. Tolkien was perfect for the post, and began there in October. Not long afterwards, Edith gave birth to their second son, Michael Hilary Reuel. Tolkien was kept very busy with the demands of his teaching and his young family, but he also found time to work on **academic** writing, to compose poetry – which was occasionally published in magazines – and to continue with stories for *The Silmarillion*. In 1924, the university made Tolkien a Professor. At only 32, he was young for this distinguished title.

This is what Leeds University looked like when Tolkien taught there.

FIND OUT MORE...

Tolkien began a students' Viking Club with another teacher, Eric Valentine Gordon. At meetings, they drank beer, read **sagas** in Anglo-Saxon and Old Icelandic, and sang rude songs they made up in these ancient languages!

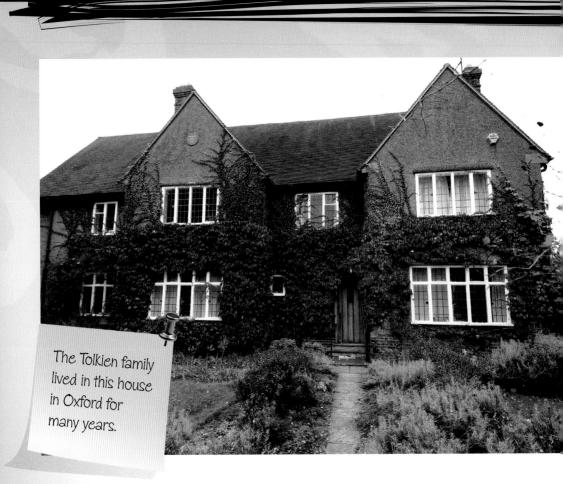

The Tolkien family lived in this house in Oxford for many years.

Return to Oxford

In November 1924, John and Edith's third son was born, and they named him Christopher Reuel. Soon afterwards, Tolkien was invited to take up the position of Professor of Anglo-Saxon at his old university, Oxford. He decided to move back to the city he knew and loved so well. The Tolkiens were to live in Northmoor Road, Oxford, for around twenty years. Everyone was delighted when a daughter completed the family in 1929: Priscilla Mary Reuel.

Tolkien the family man

Tolkien's days in Oxford were a bustle of teaching, working on academic writings and *The Silmarillion*, and marking exam papers for other universities to earn extra money. However, he also enjoyed having fun with his children. He played noisy games with them, and went for long countryside walks, boat trips on the local river Cherwell, visits to the theatre, and holidays at the seaside.

Stories for the children

Tolkien discovered he had a flair for inventing stories to entertain his children. These included tales about a red-headed boy who had adventures through a cuckoo clock, and an unstoppable villain named Bill Stickers. Tolkien began to write some of his stories down. For example, *Roverandom* was about a dog that was turned into a toy by a wizard. He also wrote tales about his son Michael's Dutch doll, Tom Bombadil, and *Mr Bliss*, about a man's adventures in his new car. This was written after Tolkien bought his first car in 1932. Tolkien also sometimes drew colourful pictures to illustrate his stories.

FIND OUT MORE...

Each December, Tolkien sent his children a special, illustrated letter from Father Christmas. It was filled with news about his polar bear lodger, snowman gardener, elf secretary, and troublesome goblin neighbours. These letters are now collected together in a book, called *Letters from Father Christmas*.

Tolkien's first car was a Morris Cowley like this one.

Inspiration from friends

Tolkien developed a close set of friends among his colleagues at Oxford University. He began "the Coalbiters' Club", where members met to read and discuss the exciting story-poems of Old Icelandic literature. Then Tolkien became part of a small group of friends who met to share thoughts on their own writing.

The group called themselves "the Inklings" and they usually met on Tuesday mornings in the Eagle and Child pub in the centre of Oxford, and on Thursday evenings in the college rooms of a university teacher called C.S. Lewis. C.S. Lewis became a particularly close friend of Tolkien's, and the two often met up on their own to discuss each other's writing. Tolkien's main focus was on legends for *The Silmarillion*, but he worked on other writing too, such as poetry, and a time-travel story called *The Lost Road*.

C.S. Lewis also became a well-known author. He wrote a famous series of stories called *The Chronicles of Narnia*.

A story in print

Some time around 1930, Tolkien was marking exam papers when a line popped into his head. He jotted it down: "In a hole in the ground there lived a hobbit." Tolkien developed a mythical adventure story from it, complete with drawings. He read it to his children, and also showed it to C.S. Lewis and a student called Elaine Griffiths. Elaine Griffiths told a publisher friend about it, and the publisher asked to see it. As a result, *The Hobbit* was published in the UK in September 1937 and soon afterwards in the USA. It quickly became a children's best-seller!

INSIDE INFORMATION

Tolkien once wrote: "I am in fact a hobbit in all but size". He gave his hobbit characters his own personal likes: gardens and trees, pipe-smoking, plain food, and getting up late!

Today, many fans of J.R.R. Tolkien and C.S. Lewis go to visit The Eagle and Child pub in Oxford.

What next for hobbits?

Tolkien's publisher, Stanley Unwin, was keen to publish a follow-up story to *The Hobbit*. Tolkien had linked the landscapes, creatures, and legends of *The Hobbit* into the world of *The Silmarillion*, so he showed Unwin the huge manuscript which he had worked on for so long. Unwin thought the work was very promising, but would not be what hobbit fans wanted. Tolkien also showed Unwin some of his other children's stories, such as a tale called *Farmer Giles of Ham*. Unwin said that again, these were good – but not about hobbits. Tolkien began to plan a brand new tale. It centred around a magic ring possessed by the main character of *The Hobbit*, Bilbo Baggins. Tolkien eventually called it *The Lord of the Rings*. He ended up working on it for twelve years.

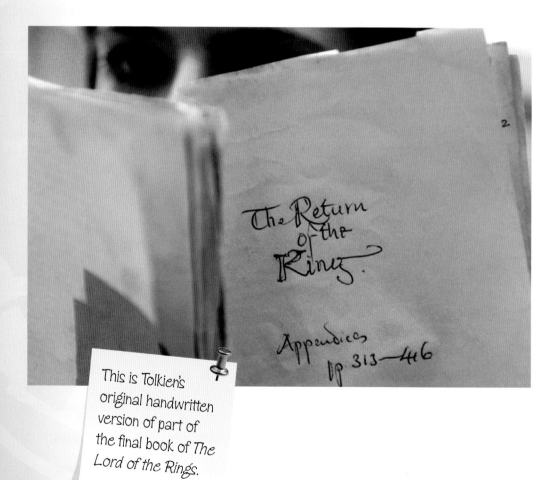

This is Tolkien's original handwritten version of part of the final book of *The Lord of the Rings*.

These are some of Tolkien's friends from the Inklings, including C.S. Lewis (second from the right).

A writing marathon

Tolkien took so long writing *The Lord of the Rings* that Unwin published *Farmer Giles of Ham* anyway, in 1949. By 1950, Tolkien felt that *The Lord of the Rings* was more or less ready. However, the story was so lengthy that Unwin wanted to publish it in three books. Tolkien was not happy with the idea to split his story up into separate books. He was also upset because Unwin still did not want to publish *The Silmarillion*. Tolkien tried another publisher, but in the end had to accept Unwin's wishes. The three books, called *The Fellowship of the Ring*, *The Two Towers*, and *The Return of the King*, finally appeared in 1954 and 1955.

INSIDE INFORMATION

Tolkien read *The Lord of the Rings* to the Inklings. C.S. Lewis admired it, but told Tolkien he did not like certain bits, particularly the poems. When C.S. Lewis read Tolkien his *Chronicles of Narnia* stories in turn, Tolkien did not like them at all.

A world-famous writer

Just before *The Lord of the Rings* was published, Tolkien and Edith moved to a new home: 76 Sandfield Road in Headington, Oxford. The couple were in their early sixties and their children had grown up and left home. Tolkien expected to carry on teaching for a while and then have a quiet retirement. However, sales of *The Lord of the Rings* in both the UK and the USA rapidly grew, and the story was translated into many languages.

By the time Tolkien retired from the university at the age of 67, he found himself rich from the books. His days were hectic with interviews, replying to invitations to give talks and attend book signings, and answering sack-loads of fanmail.

Unwelcome interruptions

Tolkien often received phone calls from fans who had gone to great lengths to find out his number. Unfortunately, these were often in the middle of the night, because the fans were from countries far away in a different time zone. Other fans tracked down Tolkien's home address and lurked outside his house with cameras, trying to photograph him through the windows. He could hardly find the time or privacy to write.

Despite all the interruptions, Tolkien worked hard to complete and **revise** the book he had been working on all his adult life: *The Silmarillion*. Allen & Unwin were now keen to publish it after all. However, he often had to break off to work on academic writings. Tolkien only managed to finish shorter works of fiction, such as *The Adventures of Tom Bombadil and Other Verses* (1962), *Tree and Leaf* (1964), and *Smith of Wootton Major* (1967).

FIND OUT MORE...

Tolkien valued readers' letters very highly and took each one seriously. He sometimes wrote two or three versions of a reply before he felt happy enough to send it.

Bournemouth was a very popular seaside town when Tolkien lived there.

Final years

In 1968, when Tolkien was 76 and Edith was 79 and in ill health, the couple decided to move to a smaller house. They found a bungalow in one of their favourite holiday places, Bournemouth. Tolkien managed to keep his whereabouts a secret, to stop fans from turning up expectedly. He wanted to be interrupted less so he could have more time for writing.

Just three years later, Edith died. Tolkien returned to Oxford, where Merton College gave him a set of rooms in a college house. Friends and family often came to visit. After a couple of years, in 1973, Tolkien became ill with a **stomach ulcer** and died. He was 81. Sadly, Tolkien never saw the publication of *The Silmarillion*, his greatest passion and life's work. His son Christopher organised this several years after Tolkien's death, in 1977.

TOLKIEN'S WRITING

Tolkien found it easiest to write at night, when all his daytime duties were out of the way. Tolkien's days were a whirl of nipping around Oxford on his bicycle. He was a deeply religious man who started the day at least once a week by going to church. Then he might teach a student in his study at home, or go to the Examination Schools on the High Street to give a group lecture. He also sometimes had meetings with the other university English teachers, at Merton College. Then there was time spent with his family, having meals, helping his children with homework or telling them bedtime stories. When everyone was asleep, and there was peace and quiet at last, he sat down to write. He often worked well into the early hours of the morning.

Tolkien's poetry

Tolkien often wrote poems, although not many were ever published. He composed his poetry in ancient styles, one of which is **alliterative** verse, where the same letters are repeated several times in a line. Can you spot the alliteration in these lines Tolkien wrote from a poem about a hero called Turin and a dragon?

"On manhood's threshold he was mighty holden in the wielding of weapons; and in weaving song he had a minstrel's mastery..."

FIND OUT MORE...

Alliterative verse was composed for reading out loud. Ancient stories often used alliteration because they were passed on through speaking and in song, rather than being written down. Tolkien's students were amazed when he read great alliterative poems like *Beowulf* to them. In normal conversation, he had a muffled speaking voice. But when Tolkien performed poetry, he was loud, clear, and dramatic.

How Tolkien liked to work

When Tolkien was writing academic work he sometimes used a large Hammond typewriter. It had different typefaces, one of which had special Anglo-Saxon letters. However, when Tolkien worked on stories and poems, he liked to write them out **longhand**. He was a perfectionist and spent literally years going over his stories making corrections and adding indexes, glossaries, and notes.

INSIDE INFORMATION

Tolkien once said that a story "grows like a seed in the dark out of the leaf-mould of the mind: out of all that has been seen or thought or read, that has long ago been forgotten, descending into the deeps…"

Tolkien loved to relax outdoors in Oxford's Botanic Gardens, where he had a favourite tree.

THE SILMARILLION

The plot

The Silmarillion is a book of elf legends which provide the history of the world in which *The Hobbit* and *The Lord of the Rings* take place. It is divided up into five parts:

The Ainulindale............... tells of the creation of the world
The Valaquenta............... describes spirits
The Quenta Silmarillion .. tells the tale of three stolen elf jewels
The Akallabeth................ tells of the downfall of Men
Of the Rings of Power .... tells of events leading up to the story of *The Lord of the Rings*.

Main characters

Iluvatar.......... elf name for the first and mightiest being: "God", the creator of the world
the Ainur....... powerful spirits. Fourteen go to live in the world and become known as the Valar
Melkor.......... fifteenth Valar who turns evil and becomes the first Dark Lord
the Maiar ...... spirits whose descendants include the evil wizard, Saruman, and the good wizard, Gandalf
Men .... created by Iluvatar. Men live first on the island kingdom of Numenor, then in two nations: Gondor and Arnor.
Elves............. created by Iluvatar
Dwarves .... created by a Valar, given life by Iluvatar.

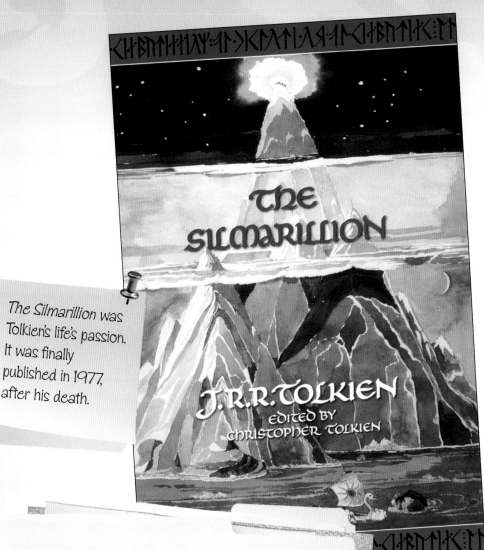

The Silmarillion was Tolkien's life's passion. It was finally published in 1977, after his death.

THE SILMARILLION

J.R.R. TOLKIEN

EDITED BY
CHRISTOPHER TOLKIEN

INSIDE INFORMATION

Tolkien spent all his life working out every tiny detail of his mythological world, as if the stories truly were ancient history. He imagined how the legends could have been handed down through generations and finally written down. Tolkien said that it happened like this: Bilbo Baggins collected ancient legends together from the memories of elves, as well as from a few rare old books. Bilbo wrote them all down in red leather notebooks. Bilbo and Frodo wrote down their own exploits too. Parts of these notebooks were later copied and eventually told separately as *The Silmarillion*, *The Hobbit*, and *The Lord of the Rings*.

THE HOBBIT

Main characters

Bilbo Baggins .... a hobbit – and a reluctant hero

Gandalf .... an old, very powerful, good wizard

Dwalin, Balin, Kili,
  Fili, Dori, Nori,
  Ori, Oin, Gloin,
  Bifur, Bofur,
  and Bombur .... a company of twelve dwarves

Thorin Oakenshield ... noble dwarf leader

William, Bert, Tom .... three bandit trolls

Elrond .... noble, wise half-elf, who lives in the
                            hidden elf realm of Rivendell

the Great Goblin .... ruler of the cruel goblins who live in
                            mountain mines. Elves call goblins "orcs".

Gollum .... small, slimy creature who secretly
                            possesses a gold ring of powerful magic

the Wargs .... a band of wild, evil wolves

the Lord of
  the Eagles .... noble-hearted bird ruler who lives
                            in the Misty Mountains

Beorn .... man who can take the shape of
                            a giant, fearsome bear

the spiders
  of Mirkwood .... giant, flesh-eating creatures

the Elven King .... ruler of the Wood-elves

Smaug .... mighty dragon with an enormous
                            hoard of dwarf treasure

Bard .... man who kills Smaug and lays claim
                            to his treasure

The plot

Bilbo Baggins lives in a quiet part of Middle-Earth called the Shire. One day a wizard and thirteen dwarves arrive at his door. They whisk Bilbo off on a journey into the east, to win back the ancient treasure hoard which once belonged to the dwarf kings. The treasure is now guarded by a terrible dragon called Smaug. The travellers battle all sorts of evil forces, before Bilbo, who the dwarves have chosen to be their burglar, has to face Smaug. During the adventures, Bilbo accidentally finds a magic gold ring, which is far more important than he imagines.

INSIDE INFORMATION

Bilbo Baggins' home is called Bag End. This was what people called a farm in Worcestershire belonging to Tolkien's Aunt Jane. Tolkien based Bilbo's village of Hobbiton on another real place: his beloved childhood home of Sarehole.

The Hobbit was first published in 1937.

THE LORD OF THE RINGS

Main characters

Hobbits:
    Bilbo Baggins .... now a very elderly hobbit
    Frodo Baggins............ Bilbo's much younger cousin and heir
    Samwise Gamgee .... Bilbo and Frodo's gardener
    Meriadoc Brandybuck (Merry)
      and Peregrin Took
      (Pippin) .... Frodo's loyal friends

Elves:
    Elrond .... now Lord of Rivendell
    Arwen .... Elrond's brave, beautiful daughter
    Legolas .... a Mirkwood elf prince
    Galadriel .... Lady of the Lothlorien elves

Humans:
    Aragorn .... nobleman of Numenor
    Boromir and Faramir .. noblemen of Gondor
    Lord Denethor............ Boromir and Faramir's father
    King Theoden.............. ruler of the people of Rohan
    Wormtongue .... King Theoden's evil advisor
    Eomer and Eowyn ..... King Theoden's nephew and niece

Others:
    Gandalf .... the great, good wizard from *The Hobbit*
    Gimli........................... a dwarf, son of Gloin from *The Hobbit*
    Gollum .... creature who we discover was once a
                                            hobbit called Smeagol
    Treebeard .... a type of ancient tree-spirit called an Ent
    Saruman .... powerful wizard who has turned to evil
    Sauron........................ the mighty, evil Dark Lord of Mordor

The plot of *The Fellowship of the Ring*

Bilbo mysteriously disappears at his eleventy-first birthday party, leaving Frodo alone at Bag End. Nine years later, Gandalf arrives and explains that dark forces threaten the world. Sauron is searching for a magical gold ring that Bilbo left to Frodo. Frodo must travel deep into Sauron's realm and destroy the ring in the volcano, Orodruin. He and his friends set off on their perilous quest.

They are joined by Aragorn, Gimli, Legolas, Boromir, and Gandalf himself, and are helped by the elves of Rivendell and Lothlorien. However, they face continual terrifying dangers, and Gandalf is lost in the Mines of Moria. Boromir shockingly tries to steal the Ring, and Frodo secretly decides he must carry on alone. Sam realizes and catches up with Frodo just in time, and the two leave the rest of the group behind.

The Fellowship of the Ring was published in 1954.

The plot of *The Two Towers*

Boromir defends his friends from attacking orcs and dies honourably – although Merry and Pippin are captured by the orcs. They later escape and seek help from Treebeard and the Ents.

Meanwhile, Aragorn, Legolas, and Gimli meet Gandalf again in Rohan. With King Theoden's warriors of Rohan, they fight a huge orc army at the fortress of Helm's Deep. They then travel on to attack Sauron's ally, Saruman, at Isengard. They find him already crushed, due to the brave actions of Merry, Pippin, and the Ents.

Frodo and Sam determinedly head towards Mordor. Gollum betrays them and leads them into the lair of a monster spider. Orcs capture Frodo and take him into a guardtower on the edge of Mordor. Sam is left helpless outside.

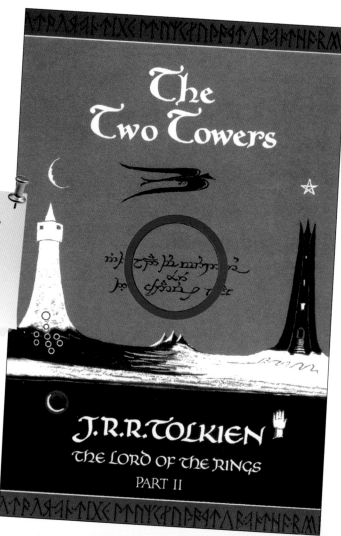

The Two Towers was published in 1954.

The plot of *The Return of the King*

Gandalf and Pippin ride like the wind on the magical horse, Shadowfax. They head for Boromir's home, Minas Tirith, to warn his father, Lord Denethor, about the forthcoming war with the dark forces. Theoden, Eomer, a band of warriors, and Merry ride towards battle, while Aragorn, Gimli, and Legolas take a faster, but more terrifying route – the Paths of the Dead. The fighting is bloody, but at last the evil armies are defeated.

Meanwhile, Sam courageously finds a way to rescue Frodo and they struggle on towards the fiery volcano. Will they manage to destroy the Ring before it destroys them?

The Return of the King was published in 1955.

PRIZES, PERFORMANCE, PRAISE

When Tolkien's first book, *The Hobbit*, was published in the USA in 1938, it won the New York Herald Tribune prize for the best young people's book of the season. In the late 1960s and early 1970s, *The Lord of the Rings* became very fashionable among university students in the USA. They made badges with slogans such as "Gandalf for President" and held hobbit picnics!

However, since these early, instant successes, Tolkien's works have proved timeless in their appeal and popularity. Today, academic readers as well as fans praise Tolkien's outstanding achievements. All over the world, there are books, magazines and games based on Tolkien's characters, together with countless fan clubs and **conventions**.

FIND OUT MORE...

2005 was the fiftieth anniversary of the complete publication of *The Lord of the Rings*. To celebrate the special date, the Tolkien Society held a five-day Tolkien conference and convention at Aston University in Tolkien's home city, Birmingham. Tolkien scholars, experts and fans travelled from all over the world to attend. The event was called "The Ring Goes Ever On".

Special honours

In 1972, when Tolkien was 80, the Queen honoured his outstanding work by making him a Commander of the Order of the British Empire (known as a CBE). It meant that Tolkien then had letters after his name: his full title was J.R.R. Tolkien CBE. He went to Buckingham Palace to receive his CBE medal from the Queen in person.

In 2002, Tolkien's daughter and granddaughter attended a ceremony at his former home, 20 Northmoor Road in Oxford. The city council put up a special blue plaque in honour of his links with the city.

Adaptations of Tolkien's tales

Tolkien was approached several times in his lifetime by companies who wanted to adapt his books for radio and turn them into films. *The Lord of the Rings* was broadcast as a radio **dramatization** soon after it was published. Tolkien did not like it much because he objected to adaptations of stories in general; he thought books were always best when they were just as the author wrote them.

The first film proposal for *The Lord of the Rings* was for an **animated** version. Tolkien was glad that it was never made because the script was not true to his story at all. However, since then, several film versions have been made, including a recent three-part blockbuster filmed in New Zealand, starring Elijah Wood as Frodo, Sir Ian McKellen as Gandalf, and Liv Tyler as Arwen.

The hobbit heroes from the *Lord of the Rings* movies (2001–2003).

Tolkien the language scholar

Tolkien's best-selling novels came from a deep-rooted love of ancient languages which led him to have a distinguished career as a university teacher. Students who thought that Anglo-Saxon and Medieval literature were difficult and dull changed their opinions dramatically when they heard Tolkien read it aloud. When he explained his thinking on this literature, they were inspired and passionate about it.

HAVE A GO

As a university teacher, Tolkien specialised in studying the origins and meanings of words, and spotting patterns and the development of languages. This study is known as **philology**. Tolkien was a type of "language detective". Why not try finding out where words have come from for yourself? Libraries have dictionaries of **etymology** and other reference books which will help you.

Tolkien's Elvish languages

Many experts say that Tolkien was such an oustanding philologist precisely because he did not just study languages, but he also invented them. Tolkien invented several elf languages from his early twenties onwards, and he used many elf names and words in *The Silmarillion*, *The Hobbit*, and *The Lord of the Rings*.

The languages are not just gobbledegook — they have proper grammar and spelling rules, just like real languages. Tolkien created two main elf languages: Quenya (for which he was influenced by Finnish) and Sindarin (for which he was influenced by Welsh). His Elvish languages were the main inspiration behind the mythological world in which the stories of *The Silmarillion*, *The Hobbit*, and *The Lord of the Rings* take place. It is likely that the languages came to take up as much of Tolkien's time as writing the stories themselves!

Academic accolades

Tolkien produced several academic writings which are very highly thought of to this day. These include a published lecture on the Anglo-Saxon poem *Beowulf*, essays on the language of the medieval texts *Ancrene Wisse* and *The Canterbury Tales*, and translations of ancient works including *Sir Gawain and the Green Knight*.

Tolkien was awarded many honours for his outstanding academic work. These included awards called **honorary fellowships** from Exeter College and Merton College, Oxford University, and an honorary degree from Edinburgh University. The academic award which meant the most to him was an honorary **Doctorate** of Letters from Oxford University in 1972, for his work in the study of philology.

Tolkien wore a special gown when he received his honorary Doctorate of Letters in 1972

Views in the news

Tolkien's novels won praise from many critics. These are people who write their opinions for newspapers and magazines. Book reviews are important because they help readers decide whether to spend their time and money on a story or not. Here is an example of a review for *The Silmarillion*, with some notes on how the critic has put it together. Would it encourage you to read the book?

The Silmarillion is a collection of legends that tell of a time called the Elder Days, or the First Age of the World. Other creation mythologies, such as the Old Icelandic Elda Edda, consist of the ancient stories of actual peoples from history. However, this creation mythology is entirely invented.

a summary of what kind of book it is

comparison with other works

The author, J.R.R. Tolkien, was a teacher at Oxford University who laboured all his life on this huge, magnificent vision. He is best-known for the children's classic *The Hobbit* and the worldwide best-seller *The Lord of the Rings*.

some background on the writer

The Silmarillion will captivate anyone who enjoys these works, whether young or old. The grand, poetic style may prove a challenge, but is also a great achievement following the ancient tradition of epic literature.

who the work is aimed at

the critic's opinion on whether it is a good or bad read, with clear reasons

If you enjoy tales of heroism and tragedy, mortals and magic, adventure and emotion, *The Silmarillion* is for you.

a recommendation of who the critic thinks will like the book

HAVE A GO

Why not try writing your own review of *The Hobbit*? You could give it to a friend who has not read the book and see if they go on to read it. Ask them to write a review back, recommending one of their favourite books to you.

Pieces of praise

Here are some critics' opinions on Tolkien's books:

Praise for *The Hobbit*:

> "All who love that kind of children's book which can be read and re-read by adults, should take note that a new star has appeared in this constellation."
>
> **C.S. Lewis in *The Times***

Praise for *The Lord of the Rings*:

> "...one of the most remarkable works of literature in our, or any, time."
>
> **Bernard Levin in *Truth***

> "No fiction I have read in the last five years has given me more joy."
>
> **the poet WH Auden, in *The New York Times***

Praise for *The Silmarillion*:

> "A grim, tragic, brooding and beautiful book, shot through with heroism and hope..."
>
> ***The Toronto Globe & Mail***

> "Stern, sweeping myth ... an imaginative work of staggering comprehensiveness."
>
> ***The Sydney Morning Herald***

TOLKIEN FOREVER!

Tolkien was buried with his wife, Edith. On the gravestone, following Edith's name is "Luthien" and following his own name is "Beren". These are the names of two lovers from *The Silmarillion*. You can go to see the grave for yourself at Wolvercote Cemetery in Oxford.

Many of Tolkien's fans come to his grave in Oxford, often leaving gifts such as jewellery and flowers.

Tolkien's legacy

Since Tolkien's death, many other great writers have been inspired to follow in his footsteps. For instance, we may not have had outstanding works like the "Wizard of Earthsea" books by Ursula Le Guin or the "Harry Potter" books of JK Rowling, if Tolkien had not first sparked off a lasting passion for magic, mythology, and fantasy. He brought public attention to a type of story that was often overlooked, and allowed later authors of fantasy to be taken more seriously. Tolkien was a pioneering writing hero, just as Bilbo and Frodo were pioneering hobbit heroes on their own quests.

Writing in focus

Here's what some of Tolkien's millions of fans think about him and his work:

"J.R.R. Tolkien is hobbit-forming!"

popular graffiti

"The Lord of the Rings is just magic!"

Arwen (real name Kirsty), aged thirteen, from Belfast

"Gandalf is the greatest wizard in the world."

James, aged ten, from Birmingham

TOLKIEN'S WISH LIST

Hopes...	Tolkien hardly did any travelling. He hoped one day to visit the land of many of his heroes, Iceland, but he never did.
Dreams...	Tolkien hated seeing the English landscape disappear through the the building of busy roads and the expansion of industrial towns and smoky cities. If he could have had one wish, it might have been for countryside life to stay unspoiled forever.
Ambitions...	Tolkien's lifelong ambition was to create an imagined mythology similar to the group of Finnish legends known as *The Kalevala*. He achieved this spectacularly with the writing of *The Silmarillion*, *The Hobbit*, and *The Lord of the Rings*.

43

TIMELINE

1892 John Ronald Reuel Tolkien is born on 3 January, in South Africa.

1895 Tolkien's mother takes her two young sons back to Birmingham, England, for a holiday to visit her family.

1896 Tolkien's father dies in South Africa while the rest of the family are still in England. Tolkien's mother rents a cottage at Sarehole Mill, in the countryside near Birmingham.

1904 Tolkien's mother dies. Father Francis Morgan, from the Birmingham Oratory, becomes guardian to Tolkien and his brother.

1908 Tolkien falls in love with a girl in his lodging house, Edith Bratt.

1910 Father Francis forbids Tolkien to see Edith until he is 21 years old.

1911 Tokien forms a poetry club with some friends. In the autumn, he begins studying at Exeter College, Oxford University.

1913 Tolkien turns 21. He makes contact with Edith again.

1914 Tolkien and Edith get engaged.
Tolkien wins a university award called the Skeat Prize.
World War I breaks out.

1915 Tolkien is awarded the top grade in his final university exams. He begins training as an officer in the army. He has a poem called *Goblin Feet* accepted for publication in an anthology.

1916 On 22 March, Tolkien and Edith get married. On 4 June, Tolkien is sent to fight in France. By November, Tolkien has fallen very ill. He is sent back to England to recover in hospital.

1917 Tolkien and Edith are reunited. While Tolkien recovers from his illness, he begins to write a story which he later titles *The Silmarillion*. He is to work on this for the rest of his life. In November, Tolkien and Edith's first son, John, is born.

1918 In November, World War I ends. Tolkien's closest school friends have died in the fighting. He takes a job in Oxford, working on putting together the New English Dictionary.

1919 Oxford University starts sending Tolkien students to teach.

1920 In the Autumn, Tolkien takes up the position of Reader in English Language at Leeds University.
Tolkien and Edith's second son, Michael, is born.

1922 Tolkien and a colleague begin a Viking Club at Leeds University. Tolkien also starts writing academic books.

1924 Leeds University makes Tolkien a Professor.
Tolkien and Edith's third son, Christopher, is born.

1925 Tolkien becomes Professor of Anglo-Saxon at Oxford University.

1926 Tolkien forms The Coalbiters' Club with another teacher at Oxford University, C.S. Lewis, who will later write *The Chronicles of Narnia*.

1929 Tolkien and Edith have a daughter, Priscilla.

1930 Tolkien begins writing *The Hobbit*.

1935 Tolkien, Lewis and other writer friends meet regularly to discuss their work. They call themselves the Inklings.

1937 *The Hobbit* is published. It wins the New York Herald Tribune prize for the best young people's book of the season.
Tolkien begins to write *The Lord of the Rings*.

1949 A children's story called *Farmer Giles of Ham* is published.

1954 The first two volumes of *The Lord of the Rings* are published: *The Fellowship of the Ring* and *The Two Towers*.

1955 The third and final volume of *The Lord of the Rings* is published: *The Return of the King*.

1959 Tolkien retires from university teaching.

1962 *The Adventures of Tom Bombadil* is published.

1964 A children's story called *Tree and Leaf* is published.

1967 A children's story called *Smith of Wootton Major* is published.

1968 Tolkien and Edith move to Bournemouth.

1971 Edith dies, aged 82.

1972 Tolkien returns to Oxford, living at Merton College. The Queen gives him a special honour called a CBE. Oxford University gives him an award called an honorary Doctorate of Letters.

1973 Tolkien dies on 2 September at the age of 81.

1977 *The Silmarillion* is finally published after Tolkien's death, edited by his son, Christopher.

FURTHER RESOURCES

More books to read

Bilbo's Last Song, J.R.R. Tolkien and Pauline Baynes (illustrator) (Hutchinson Children's Books, 2002)

J.R.R. Tolkien: A Biography, Humphrey Carpenter (HarperCollins, 2002)

Letters from Father Christmas: Complete and Unabridged, J.R.R. Tolkien (HarperCollins, 2004)

Audio and video

J.R.R. Tolkien's famous stories are also available as audiobooks on CD and cassette, including:

The Hobbit (BBC Audiobooks, 2002)

The Lord of the Rings (BBC Audiobooks, 2002)

The movie adaptations of *The Lord of the Rings* are available on DVD and video: *The Fellowship of the Ring*, *The Two Towers*, and *The Return of the King* (Entertainment in Video)

Websites

The publisher HarperCollins has a website all about J.R.R. Tolkien: *www.tolkien.co.uk*

The website of a society devoted to Tolkien and his work: *www.tolkiensociety.org*

Information on all things to do with Tolkien: *www.planet-tolkien.com*

Disclaimer

All the internet addresses (URLs) given in this book were valid at the time of going to press. However, due to the dynamic nature of the Internet, some addresses may have changed, or sites may have ceased to exist since publication. While the author and publishers regret any inconvenience this may cause readers, no responsibility for any such changes can be accepted by either the author or the publishers.

academic to do with education and studying

allies countries that agree to fight on the same side during a war

alliteration repeating letters several times in order to emphasize the line (lines with alliteration are called alliterative)

animated given the illusion of movement

Arthurian to do with the legendary King Arthur of Britain

Classics study of important writing from ancient civilizations, such as the Romans and Greeks

convention large meeting where fans of something or someone get together for events, displays, and discussions

doctorate highest level of academic award from a university

dramatization acted out version of a story

etymology study of words, including their meanings and where they came from

fantasy story set in an imaginary, magical world

hieroglyphics picture symbols that stand for words and letters

honorary fellowship special award from a university to mark an expert's achievements in their work

linguist someone who studies language

longhand writing on paper with a pen or pencil rather than typing

medieval period of European history which lasted from the 11th to the 15th century

middle class not one of the poorest people in society, but not one of the richest people either

miller somone who works in a grain mill

Morse code system of dots and dashes that represent letters and numbers, transmitted over radio waves to send messages

myth traditional story from early history, typically about gods, goddesses, spirits, and heroes

mythology collection of myths

philology study of languages, including how words change over time

revise look back over something in order to make improvements and corrections

saga ancient type of long story about heroes and their adventures

scholarship prize of money to help a student pay the fees for a course of study

stomach ulcer illness in which part of the stomach lining wears away

trench ditch dug on a battlefield for soldiers to shelter in and to shoot at the enemy from

trench fever illness that soldiers fighting in the trenches in World War I passed on to each other

INDEX

Titles in the *Writers Uncovered* series include:

Hardback   0 431 90626 2

Hardback   0 431 90627 0

Hardback   0 431 90628 9

Hardback   0 431 90629 7

Hardback   0 431 90630 0

Hardback   0 431 90631 9

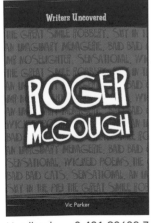

Hardback   0 431 90632 7

Hardback   0 431 90633 5

Find out about other titles from Heinemann Library on our website www.heinemann.co.uk/library